My motto:

I will try to always be sensitive to hear when the Holy Spirit speaks; for it is God who will give the words so I can bless others.

Illustrated By: Author

Published By:

Dr. Deborah Willis 2020

Printed In The U.S.A.

Deborah Lark Mitchell

Thank you For Your Support!

CONTENTS

A Well Planted Tree

A poem for a most admired person (any gender)

A well planted tree anchored and strong

will not be moved when things go wrong

Storms and winds they come and they're
gone

But this well planted tree is still hanging on

Hurricanes, tornadoes they all come
around

But this well planted tree will never fall
down

They tug, they pull, oh how they bump

But this well planted tree has got a
powerful stump

Many people come and admire this tree

She's a woman that's humble and loving
you see

God planted this tree and called it to be

Deborah Lark Mitchell the well planted tree.

Lord Have Mercy On Us!

Time is going by quickly, and time is far spent

Jesus is still calling for sinners to repent

The world is getting wiser, but weaker by the days

Young folks are getting restless and babies are getting aids

LORD HAVE MERCY ON US!

The streets are filled with murderers and people are getting mugged

Mamas they leaving their children and they also hooked on drugs

LORD HAVE MERCY ON US!

What should I do in this time of rage, when I see the world is like a movie

And I'm like an actor on the stage

Should I take my concerns and hide myself,

or should I be as a vagabond no money no
wealth

LORD HAVE MERCY ON US!

What should I do in exchange for my soul

when I see the wicked so evil, and the evil
so bold

What should I do in these last and evil days

Should I give my life to Christ who knows
all my sinful ways

Yes! I'll give my life to Christ for he knows
me by name

I'll give my life to Christ, then my life, yes
my life, will never be the same

LORD HAVE MERCY ON US!

There Stands A Rose

Dedicated To All First Ladies

Her petals all fashioned highlighted

with happiness

Even tho standing alone

she is known for her tactfulness

There stands a rose

To light up a smile and brighten a day

she sits and she flutters

God planned it that way

She's plucked, she's pulled and found

with thorns

Given away by others

yet her heart does mourn

she stands so proudly and good

Sticking close by her husband but

misunderstood

There stands a rose

Years have passed, her

mission for God she continues to do

Comforting to many, right there for you

So pluck her, pull her

give her away, she is the chosen one

God planned it that way!

There stands a rose!

The Man Who Sits In The Pulpit

In loving memory of my former pastor Suffragan Bishop W B Mitchell

The man who sits in the pulpit

The watchman of my soul

The one who teaches me the right way

Somethings just got to be told

I watch this man carefully

I feel he is a great leader

The Lord has blessed him

to be our spokesman and suffer

him not to deceive

Sometimes when I'm burden

tired, and distress

The Lord speaks thru him to tell me

Although your labor is hard my beloved one

I will and surely bless

So brothers and sisters if he had not live

This life before me, I could be lost in the

world

But since the Lord is the first partaker of

his life I know he won't forsake me

So I challenge you to be under his teaching

This one thing I can assure, you're learn all

about

Our Savior Jesus Christ Our Lord.

Mama You Saw
The Best In Me

In Loving Memory of My Mom, My Cheerleader, and My Best Teacher

Mama you saw the best in me

You prayed both day and night

Mama you saw the best in me

Until I got it right

You knew I had a special gift

that I could not explain

I had to grow and face my test

Oh God it was ordained

Mama you saw the best in me

Battle scars I have to prove

Now after all that I've been thru

My life has been renewed.

A Good Dad

In Loving Memory of my daddy

Sampson Lark Jr.

A good dad knows his kids

is his masterpiece

So he carefully guides them

in the right direction

Sacrificing his life

only for their protection

A good dad knows he can build up

or he can tear down,

That child's integrity

So he watch his words to make sure

His child would just take heed

To things he properly say and do

Hoping someday his child succeed

My Doggy Boo

The day I took you home with me

You look as though you knew

That you would be our family

We watched you as you grew

As we drove home you

didn't bark or cry

Instead you cuddled

close in my arms

You seemed a little shy

You laid your head gently on my chest

My heart did melt it's true

Yes pup I made you a promise

I'll take care of you

And I try hard to do my best

Tho Sometimes you surprise me

With all the tricks you do

I'm so glad I chose my doggy

You are the one that keeps me going

I love my doggy boo.

I'm Ringing My Bell

**In loving memory of
my sister Barbara who
lost her battle to
cancer**

They told me when I ring my bell

I would be so excited

I fought so hard

Yes I did

Thinking I could fight it

But there it was a still

Sweet voice saying

Child is gonna be

So family don't mourn to long

Rejoice, if only you could see

I'm ringing my bell

Like in my dream in

Eternity

Yes What He Saw Was Pleasing

Poem dedicated to all pastors

God looked and he saw a need in the east

And what saw was pleasing

Many coming from the east, west, north

and south

It was souls he was releasing

He knew they needed a resting place

So he gave a man a vision

To lead the people and teach them

ordinance

Yes what he saw was pleasing

He said to him if you be willing and obey

my voice

I will surely bless your land

Bless all your coming in and going out

Your cattle and your kin

So this man received his calling so proudly

and proceeded

He devoted his life and started the mission

Yes what he saw was pleasing

Now God looked down and bless his days

Promotions he did give

Because you chose this work for me

My Pastor, look and live

My Grand Baby

Came From Above

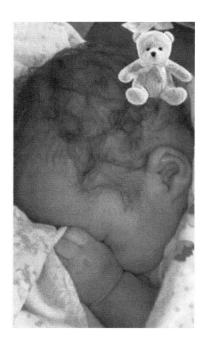

Dedicated to my granddaughter

Carter Starr Mitchell

God bless the day you were born

We all were waiting to sound our

horns

Oh the joy I felt that day

Never imagining I could feel that way

One glimpse at you, I fell in love

Because in my heart, you came from

above

Nature Is Speaking

To You

Nature teaches us the love of the Lord

It's telling us to watch the things from

above

The clouds they speak so look and listen

Thru their shapes and colors, just pay

attention

Seasons come and seasons go

Bringing a message for all to know

A time to live and a time to die

it speaks to everyone as time goes by

Nature teaches us the love of the Lord

Like trees he sees us in a special way

Trees stands with purpose and covers with

shade

So watch and pray, that's what you do

Pay attention to Nature it's speaking to you

My Sisters and Me

Sheila, Barbara, Janis, Terry, Sharon, Jackie, Paulette, & my niece LaTrese

God gave me sisters to bless my life

They are so very special they can feel my

pain

They pick me up, and put me back together

again

No one can hug like my sisters you know

They can make me laugh until I fall to the

floor

I love my sisters God gave so all can see

They are my best friends my sisters and me

In this Pandemic

A message to the world

All of sudden we were sheltered in place

But even though restrained

God has blessed us with grace

So Lord we thank you for our journey

You gave us another testimony

To recognize how bless we are

To be grateful and stop complaining

To Know within our hearts

You care for your children

And you never leave us hanging

So don't point fingers of

whose right or wrong

The race is not to

the swift or to the strong

Learn the great lesson

don't test your limits

God is talking to all of us

In this pandemic

Life

Life is not bad if you treat it right

It can be scary so get ready to fight

You got to pick your battles

And stay on your knees

For it is God my child you must

please

He is waiting for you just let him

speak

Give it to God and turn your cheek

A True Waymaker

Don't Worry about what's going on

Lift your head and square your back

Now put it in my hands

Rest my child, and trust in me

It all will come out grand

Listen to me and read my word

Be the next partaker

Remember my child I love you so

I'm your true way maker

Full of Grace

Her smile is sweet and full of taste

Yes it's _____

(Name of person)

Whose full of Grace

To look at her, we find much pleasure

Because we know she's Elder's treasure

So _____ we salute you too

(Name of person)

The _____ family truly love you

(Name of church)

Son It Will Happen

Dedicated to my sons

Dennis Jr & Darius

Son you're strong

Just trust within

You got the victory

I know you'll win

You have power

more than it seems

Don't be afraid son

live your dream

There is more of life

Than you could ever imagine

Come on be strong son

It will happen

Believe in Yourself

Why should I be bound and not believe in
me

When I got all I need to help me to
succeed

I got Jesus my Heavenly Father the one
that I adore

He's my rock and redeemer and I love him
more and more.

A Mother's Love

A Mother's love is greater than all

that's in the world

Who else you can call to be there

To get you out of hurls

Her love is unconditional

No price she charge you see

All she ask is for your respect,

love and dignity

So stop and think one day

you may lose her

In Heaven she will be

So bless her, reward her

Do all that you can do

Give her flowers while she's alive

After all you put her through

Grandparents
Are The Best

They spoil our children

and love them too

It's seem so pleasing for

them to do

Oh what a wonderful blessing

To have them around

Giving out free kisses

And never a frown

Oh Lord bless them daily

and bless their health

To Take care of their bodies

Even prosper in wealth

Let their latter be better you see

After all dear God It's all from thee

I Made The Right Decision

The other day when I got this call

I heard the voice of Jesus

Calling me to a higher place

I made the right decision

The stakes were high, I dropped it all

He showed me what to do

To walk with him and trust his word

A new vision for me too

Thank You Lord, you've been

So good to me

I made the right decision

Singing Is What I Do

When I'm feeling down and nothing
to do

I start singing that's what I do

It lifts my heart, it breaks the mold

Oh like medicine, it revives my soul

Sometimes people tell me they love
my singing

Deep down in me Joy Bells start
ringing

So when you're down and nothing to
do

Encourage yourself singing

That's what I do

Deborah Lark Mitchell 2020

My Good Blessed Man

**Dedicated to my loving and
supportive husband for 43 years**

When I look over my life

I realize you was a hidden treasure

I had to wait and trust my God

That someday you would find me

All it took was a sincere prayer

From the bottom of my heart

Believing He would send me

Someone who would love me

right from the start

So today I rejoice it was all in his plan

For it was God who chose

My sweetheart, my blessed good man

Congratulations

Sister Honey!

To my smart, beautiful and talented wife, I am so very proud of you! You did it! You have accomplished your dream, your first book. Your ministry of creative writing has blessed so many down through the years.

I am so excited about what God is doing right now in your life, and where he's taking you! I love you and my prayer for you is the Lord be with you always dear in all your endeavors!

Your loving husband, Dennis

This book was written to encourage and inspire someone who don't know their worth. Also, to esteem the person you truly admire the most who have deposited in your life such as I have had. Special thanks to my loving husband and sons, and Greater Christ Temple Church family who has always encouraged me to write this book.

And special thanks to my sister Dr. Janis Kent, who put me in the best hands, Dr. Deborah Willis

Made in the USA
Monee, IL
03 November 2020